Charikleia and I dedicate this book to each other. We ar
but like the cousins in the story, we live in different cc

Copyright © 2020 Elisavet Arkolaki, Charikleia Arko.

Translated into Spanish by Carmen Vargas Breval

For permission requests and supplementary teaching material, please write to the publisher at liza@maltamum.com www.maltamum.com

ISBN 9798708465108

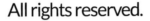

My cousin and I look alike. My aunt and uncle say we look like siblings. My mommy and daddy say we look like siblings. My grandma and grandpa, the whole family, even our friends, say we look like siblings. More like twin sisters actually, like our mothers did when they were children.

Mi prima y yo nos parecemos. Mi tía y mi tío dicen que parecemos hermanas. Mi mamá y papá dicen que parecemos hermanas. Mi abuela y mi abuelo, toda la familia, incluso nuestros amigos, dicen que parecemos hermanas. De hecho, parecemos como hermanas gemelas, como nuestras madres también se parecían cuando eran niñas.

When we were little, we lived next door to each other. To see her, all I had to do was cross the tall grass in front of our house, open the gate and enter her garden. We met every day and played all sorts of games. She was my neighbor and best friend. But then she moved.

Cuando éramos pequeñas, vivíamos una al lado de la otra. Todo lo que tenía que hacer para verla era cruzar el alto césped que había frente a mi casa, abrir la puerta y entrar en su jardín. Nos veíamos cada día y jugábamos a todo tipo de juegos. Ella era mi vecina y mi mejor amiga. Pero entonces se mudó.

Now she lives in a faraway land, and I miss her so much. Mommy said to try and find something positive no matter the circumstances. There's always something to be grateful for. And so I did. My cousin and I are very lucky. Despite the distance between us, we can still talk, play, and see each other often via video chat. We talk about everything!

Ahora ella vive en una tierra lejana y yo la echo mucho de menos. Mamá me dijo que intentara sacar algo en positivo sin importar las circunstancias. Siempre hay algo por lo que sentirse agradecidos. Así que, así lo hice. Mi prima y yo tenemos mucha suerte. A pesar de la distancia entre nosotras, aún podemos hablar, jugar y vernos de vez en cuando por videochat.

The last time we met online, she told me that it's winter and very cold there. Everything is covered in snow. She snowboards, skis, and goes ice skating with her new friends.

La última vez que nos vimos online, me contó que allí era invierno y hacía mucho frío. Todo estaba cubierto de nieve. Ella hace snowboard, esquía y va a patinar sobre hielo con sus nuevos amigos.

I told her that it's summer and very hot here.

Yo le conté que aquí era verano y hacía mucho calor.

I swim and snorkel every day with our old friends, and we watch the most beautiful fish underwater.

Yo nado y hago snorkel todos los días con nuestros viejos amigos, y bajo el agua vemos los peces más bonitos.

Then, we spoke about animals. She said mammals with fur white as snow live in the northern part of her country: polar bears, arctic foxes, seals.

Después, hablamos de animales. Ella dijo que los mamíferos de pelo blanco como la nieve viven en la parte norte de su país: osos polares, zorros árticos, focas.

I had hoped she would also talk about monkeys, but it turns out they don't live there at all!

Yo tenía la esperanza de que también hablara de los monos, ¡pero resulta que allí no hay!

She also asked about her pet which stayed behind with me. I answered that her cat is in very good hands and gets lots of cuddles and kisses.

Ella también me preguntó por su mascota, quien se quedó conmigo. Le contesté que su gato está en buenas manos y recibe muchos besos y arrumacos.

And I still go to the park on Sundays, and feed the ducks we both love so much.

Y yo todavía voy al parque los domingos, y le doy de comer a los patos que tanto nos gustaban a las dos.

Then, my cousin used some foreign words, and in an accent, I didn't recognize. I felt confused. She said she couldn't remember how to say "mountain", "rocks", and "river", and that she now talks more in her father's language.

Después, mi prima dijo algunas palabras extranjeras, y con acento, que yo no reconocí. Me sentí confundida. Me dijo que no podía acordarse de cómo decir 'montaña', 'piedras' y 'río', y que ahora habla más en el idioma de su padre.

She explained that sometimes it's hard for her to find the right words in our language. I told her I understand. I'm also learning another language at school, and it should be fun to compare words from our different languages.

Me explicó que, a veces, le resulta difícil encontrar las palabras correctas en su propio idioma. Yo le dije que la entendía. También estoy aprendiendo otro idioma en el colegio, y quizá podría ser divertido comparar palabras de nuestros diferentes idiomas.

That is how we came up with the "Word Swap" painting game. My cousin painted a cactus, and then both of us said the word out loud. "Cactus" sounds the same in all our languages!

Así es cómo se nos ocurrió el juego de pintar de 'Intercambio de palabras'. Mi prima pintó un cactus, y después las dos dijimos la palabra en voz alta. ¡Cactus suena igual en nuestros idiomas!

Her parents overheard us and joined the conversation. My aunt is a linguist and she told us that there are currently over 7,000 known spoken languages around the world! My uncle is a language teacher and he challenged us to swap a couple more words. We kept on going for a while with words like "flower", "water", "love", and "friendship".

Sus padres nos escucharon y se unieron a la conversación. Mi tía es lingüista y nos contó que, actualmente, hay más de 7.000 idiomas hablados y conocidos en el mundo. Mi tío es profesor de idiomas y nos retó a intercambiar un par de palabras más. Seguimos jugando un poco más con palabras como 'flor', 'agua', 'amor' y 'amistad'.

Next time we video chat, I will share this painting I made for her. I would like to swap the word "home".

La próxima vez que hagamos un videochat, le enseñaré este dibujo que hice para ella. Me gustaría intercambiar la palabra 'hogar'.

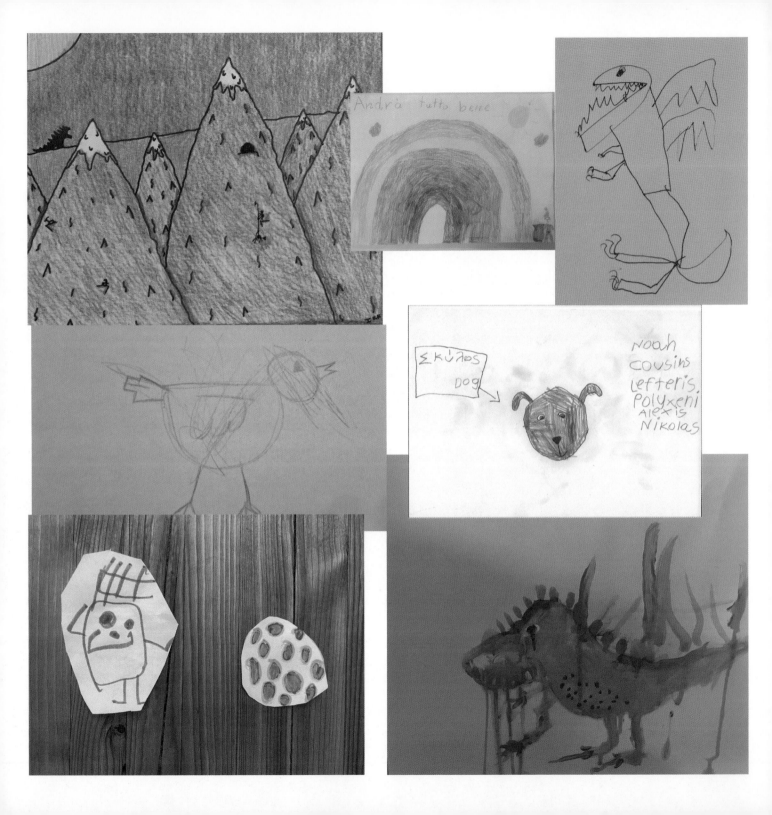

# The Word Swap Game - Meet the children!

Erik, Nelly, Iason, Iria, Sadiq, Tariq, Vincent, Rukeiya, Lea, Hector, Victor, Orestis, Odysseas, Noah, Polyxeni, Lefteris, Alexis, Nikolas, Iahn, Chloe, Ioli, Rea, Nicolas, Sveva, Giuseppe, Zafiris, Dimitris, Periklis, Vaggelis, Andrea, Zaira, Philippos, Nefeli, Baby, George, Emmanuela, Mason, Ethan, Elijah, Oliver, Athina, Apolonas, Alexandros, John, Martina, Steffy, Thanos, Nikolai, Areti, Nikolai, Nina, Nicol, Joni, Mia, Emma, Stella, Artemis, Mirto, Antonis, Nicolas, Mihalis, Katerina, Nikos, Alexis, Liam, Olivia, Noah, William, Ava, Jacob, Isabella, Patricia, Hannah, Matthew, Ashley, Samantha, Maureen, Leanne, Kimberly, David, Marie, Vasilis, Yiannis, Kyra, Joakim, Alexander, Nikolas, Ellie, Sebastian, Sophie, Sabina, Stepan, Vasilis, Yiannis, Kyra, Youjin, Sejin, Okito, Magdalini, Nicoletta, Efimia, Di, Bia, Timo, Vittoria.

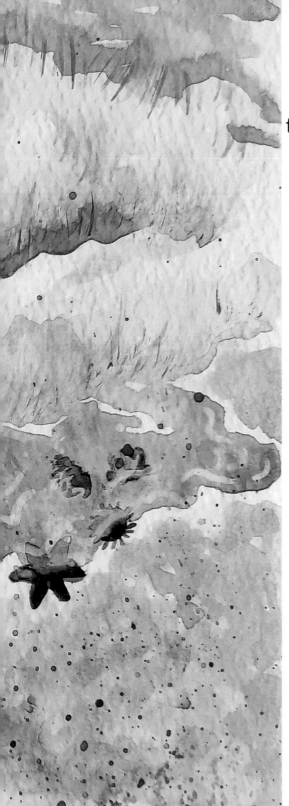

Dear Child,

I hope you enjoyed this story. If you'd also like to play the "Word Swap" game, ask an adult to help you, if needed, to write down your favorite word, and then draw or paint it. Your guardian can send me your painting via email at liza@maltamum.com, and I'll share it with other parents and children in my Facebook group "Elisavet Arkolaki's Behind The Book Club".

Dear Grown-up,

If you feel this book adds value to children's lives, please leave an honest review on Amazon or Goodreads. A shout-out on social media and a tag #CousinsForeverWordSwap would also be nothing short of amazing. Your review will help others discover the book, and encourage me to keep on writing. Visit eepurl.com/dvnij9 for free activities, printables and more.

Forever grateful, thank you!

All my best,
Elisavet Arkolaki

Printed in Great Britain
by Amazon